WHISPER HEAD

POEMS BY

CRAIG LEFEBVRE

Print ISBN: 978-1-7349058-4-7
E-Book ISBN: 978-1-7349058-5-4

Published by Dimensional Healings

Concept and design: Craig Lefebvre

Edited by:
Melissa Lefebvre
Jill Behme Conaway
Kathleen Schurman

Creative Director: John Chadziewicz

Book cover & layout: Word-2-kindle.com

For Ann, Jill and Jim

Contents

Introduction

When you write poetry, you gotta want to rip out your own heart and throw it to the floor and show it who's boss. The inner conflict of the mind gets played out when I sit down in front of the keyboard, but only if I'm in the mood. The impetus for writing can be very simple or totally complex. Spirit might whisper in my ear some days and then the next day nothing, or I might just be walking up the stairs and a verse pops into my head. But what I like most is when they come to me, those departed souls, the ones who tell me stories and show me the parts of the world that I have failed to pay attention to or couldn't quite understand.

The older I get, the more I listen to those voices now, the ones who told me to write about my dreams and the ones who accused me of liking to be sad while refusing to get out of bed in the morning. Any thought in my mind can be turned into poetry. But is it any good? Well that is up to you to decide, and I'll just keep on typing away while you read. Please enjoy the imagery of my childhood, my daydreams, my nightmares, my virginity and my spiritual awakening, as they are just whispers in my head.

ACT 1.

Summer

Solitude attitude

A hundred miles from nowhere
I sit alone at a wooden table
a table I built with these two hands
alone in my solitude, here I sit,
alone as a writer

Here is where it happens, I create
The thoughts transverse the mind
and it is here, that I wage war
upon myself, the solitary figure
in a battle of wills

Alone, I fight with no one but the self
One solitary figure, sitting in silence
Always in tribulation, fighting with
lost thoughts and feelings, the days
of my youth which are to be
past, dead and gone

Only now, I sit here as a writer
the war is heating up and I see myself
all aflame, walking through my childhood
walking through my sorrows, a broken heart
standing alone in a rain

Youth, a vocation

There I was, in the hot evening of summer
in a very far off place with light winds
She was no stranger to me, and I was no stranger to her
I did kiss her drunken lips that night, in turn so she kissed mine
How awkward it had felt under these sedated circumstances,
how awkward to interfere with the presence of my dear friend

Sometimes, it isn't the truth that can be said, as our minds are
much too afraid to speak their truths. How often do we float
through these lives headed towards an earthly grave and
never accept the truth of that which is before us? How
often is it that I sit and just wonder, thinking we are characters
of ourselves in the making of shadows that we do
walk in, from time to time. Just as shadows, we do walk in.

What of now

Specific ingredients, what are they
How is it that they are
How is it that they've become

Fingering through the old photo albums
What are they, other than lapses in time
Who made it possible for this to be

And what of time
where has it been and gone off to
For if growing up were so hard
why do the memories seem so fond to me

These memories
they're who I've become
Undress me
remove my cloak of thoughts
I'm bare memory, that's all

Walt W.

Walking through the fields
of high grass
Passing by deep graves
stained in the blood
of our Constitution
Where we laid to rest
all of our fallen brethren

The landscape is licked
by the flames of the
setting sun
We are the fallen
walking as ghosts do
we are the fallen
reflecting in times of deep change
in a country just being born

Then I leaned down, to see so closely
and maybe smell the last breath
of a fallen brother,
and does he still speak?

Maybe it's to know
and
maybe it's to know
if he is to whisper
to me, one more time...
a last possible word
For we are the fallen

But, you may just see us
as a whisper to a ghost
passing by a grave
singing the songs
of our freedom
the long forgotten
Blue's and Grey's

To Pablo

I'll have coffee,
then I shall have tea

It's too early to use words
now that my fingers are at play
They run over the rough
and ragged pages here

Maybe I too will roam
through my thoughts for
a long while
hoping to find
old memories
to use in verse

Yes, that is what I'll find
for you, just for you
old memories
that are like sunken ships
grown over with the ocean's
desire, as a desire will hold
something very close
and deep. So deep have
I buried these memories

Then like tiny air bubbles
they will start to sing
as they rise to the surface
where they once again
gain new life, I breathe
Be free, says the ocean's breath
alas I have called you all away

The Wave

I see you as I see myself
Stirred, raw and naked
alive and well, living in
the matrix of a dream,
in a sequence of time space
lapsing over me like a wave
with its milky white foam
washing ashore for the last
time before the tide sets
on another day, another
lifetime. I do hear the bells
toll now, I do hear you sing
my destiny. Ready, here I
am, as I will always be.

The trail home

In the woods where we play
there is only the silence
of trees, that only pretend
to love the sun

Beneath our feet is a symphony
of crushing fall leaves
and
each step takes us both closer
to a place we call our home

It's a cold autumn day
and lunch,
today it's at your house
with
tomato soup and grilled cheese
but look out because
your mom always burns it!

The Stairs

My long-johns have holes
at the knees and
it was true, we were inventive
and creative, with any given
box, basket, blanket, pillow,
or found object

There were many days where
it seemed to endlessly rain
These rain-soaked days brought us
to such great acts of imagination
and creativity

Most often, we took it
we took it to the stairs
And yes,
It was on those stairs
that we took to our flights
of lunacy

We rode in our found objects
and in all manner of things
like:
in boxes
in laundry baskets
on blankets
on sleeping bags
garbage bags too
and when they weren't watching
we even used our winter sled

Now, here I sit writing
on a rain soaked day
lost perhaps, but not forgotten
staring out the window
I'm still a child looking at the holes
in the knees, only this time
an old pair of dungarees

The Gardener

And there he stood
dropping his work gloves
on the shed floor
The world was at his feet
and with two dusty hands
he did then deliver a clap
so the dirt was falling
back to the earth
the place where he planted,
planted seeds of wisdom

As he stood there, before the dirt
and there she did lay, with
a swollen belly, and ripe bosom
ready
to give birth once more

She, she is the mother
to our lives, nevermore thankful
he nodded in appreciation to her
with her swollen breast
where the seeds were given
so new life could form once more

Whisper Head

It was there in the dirt
it was there where the real truth lived
For the Earth, she is always honest
If mad, we get thunder
when appreciative, we get rainbows
It's true to me, as it is honest
for nothing is more true
and life giving
than the soil of earth

They went to Nam

All my friends' fathers were in Nam
so at least it seemed to me
growing up

It was a long list of men too
my uncle, Tony, Ray and Cliff...
I've had the honor to know them
too

It was Casey and Dave's dads
who were helicopter mechanics
My uncle a radio operator
Dean's father even had a wooden leg
-taken off by shrapnel

I grew up with stories of Charlie
and how some of our good men had to pay
They paid with their body parts
and nightmares of
muzzle flashes, mortar shells
and memories of
cold nights sitting in the mud and rain

They returned as heroes
but couldn't wear their uniforms
not unless you wanted to get heckled
and this is how we treated them

They were all good men to me
I'm sure they fought with dignity
and saw things I can't ever imagine

All my friends' fathers were in Nam
they fought for me, so that, here I am

Sophia

The child in me
recognizes the child in you
I am here, your father
a father of life
both of breath and in blood
the kin of man

As I live and breathe
it is for you, so it is
all for you
my child

I am not the blood
of my past
but I am
the blood of you

Our heritage is given forth
to ourselves on this day
I call to our kindred spirits
so they join us and they feast
as we do live a life of joy

I tell you of my past
mostly the good things too
Let the dark stay in the dark
I can not change those things
the things I left behind
but in this moment
you can surely hear my bated breath

Let me sing to you once more
the world is yours! I say…
the world is yours
and only yours
to be as you make of it

Simple things

Sometimes,
it is the most simple of things
that mean so much to me

For example, a mug
a birthday gift too
It said my name on it
and right below it
Super Star

It was gifted to me on my
sixth or seventh birthday
and now I can't even remember
but it was nice to know
that I was in fact loved
by somebody

Loved, as my world
became so fractured
by my mothers drinking
and then my parents'
bitter divorce

Loved by and whom
the innocence of a now
very insecure child
stands before you

The mug was insignificant
but so are a lot of things
and that doesn't make them
any less valuable
as all I wanted to know
was that I was loved

Quarantine

We're all so bored now
that we've resorted to picking
the many pieces of paper
from our office floor

I don't even remember if we spilled them
they are like the many pieces
of a puzzle, but a really cheap one
the kind you get from a dollar store

The puzzle that makes you scream out
in glorious frustration
and out of spite too,
so you just walk away

And

No! I cried, it's missing a piece
come on! Really?
And this one is so misshapen
it doesn't even fit
Dear Lord, the humanity
but look now, the house
she is so clean...

Payphone

I grew up in a time
called the 80's
where we actually talked to people
on the phone and over coffee
or
maybe sent a postcard or two
when on vacation
...and now?

Something has been lost in the world of today
There is a serious lack of intimacy
and lack of physical connection,
...wouldn't you say?

I grew up in a time
when we had a mustard yellow rotary phone
The dial was turned one number at a time
clicking as it worked back and forth,
as it went.
We memorized phone numbers too
...how many do you know?

It was nice to just call someone up
and have a nice chat and maybe gossip
about the neighbors and who is
dating who.
...what is texting?

I grew up in a time
where there were no cell phones

and high-tech mobile devices
It was the time of analog everything
and we were yet to be immersed
into this technocratic world
that we live in today
Can I come inside and use your phone?

So way back when,
If I wanted to get a ride home
from my mom and dad
it was through the humble payphone
The not so smart phone...

I grew up in a time
where we actually used our
quarters, dimes and nickels
to buy shit, honest and for real

I grew up in a time called the 80's
It was all New Wave, Punk Rock,
Jams, Miami Vice and Cocaine

We too were missing the debit cards,
ATMs, mobile payments, seat belts,
helmets, helicopter parents,
and instant communication gratification
It was missing all these things
and it was the most amazing decade

This was my first decade, where I first learned
to kiss, ride a bike, fly a kite, drink a beer,
do a kick flip on my skate board,
and take incredible risks...
just for the fun of it.

Nutmegger

Hear me now...
this is the sound of my voice
with its trepidations and inconsistencies, too

This is my tone, my accent free
In my own voice you will hear
nothing of its likeness
in the way you should think of me

Smell the copper on my breath
there are many nuances there
the reflection of a New Englander
yes I am, and I lie somewhere
in between New York and Boston
but never am I one before the other

A child to nature all prostrate
with pine sap on my hands
and in my hair just the same
My voice it calls, it calls and
it calls

Hear me from summer
hear me from winter
As I stand in a barren field
frozen in a time

This moment of my voice,
and I will do it justice
even as I quiver in
the cold, walking
through the woods
stepping over branches
crunching acorns beneath
my child-like feet

Not quite there

I always loved dogs growing up
I always wanted a dog
and I always asked for a dog
too

He says no!
because I was allergic
or some bullshit like that
but that never did stop me

The guy across the street had a Husky
and everyday I'd stop to say hi
with handfuls of gray and white fur
as it was so friendly,
left there, tied to a tree?
And then I returned back home
full of hives...
Oh, my allergies
my fucking allergies

Then one day my dad got remarried
that bitch came with cats!

My Hero

You cast a long shadow on me
such a long shadow
A bit misunderstood perhaps
but all great men are
Sometimes in our lives
we look to one another
for both love and support
and most definitely
a helping hand

You'd take me on walks to the corner store
a place I could buy five cent candy
On the way to, there was a rock
placed at the end of a driveway
painted a stark white
you'd take my hand most carefully
and I would jump from that rock
the absolute highlight of my day

Now, I'm too out of breath
to even say thank you
and for all that, you are my hero
not because you saved me
but simply because
you were there for me

Muddy River

From a far-off field
we could just barely
see the street

It was in these fields
where we created and
executed our games
of high imagination

The walk to those fields
took us deep through the woods
A place of vacancy
no homes, no parents, no regrets
just muddy feet and a frozen river

Looking back now,
they built homes on my
treasured oasis
The kind of homes that
take up far to much space
with too much grass
and empty rooms
begging for furniture

You may have bought these homes
but I really own them,
in my imagination
as I'm still standing there
with my muddy feet

Lov'r

Lover be warned of me
that I am not full of grande
gestures and high talk
nor am I of the flashy things
that may give you sway
towards me as your man

No, I am a simpler man
for you to see:
One who asks for you to honor me
One who knows that I can not live
unless you are supporting me
One who graces the world with words
as only you can believe in me

Think not of heavy aspirations
I will be here for you
day after day after day, like the
steady tick of an old clock

I am not throwing out
false pretenses of myself either
as I capture that look in your eyes
but rather I sing of all the little things,
as it is the little things I love about you
and it is in the greatest admiration
that I most simply say, thank you.

Just say No

What child is there
that does not like candy
and as a child, there
in the 80's
I was left out too late
and to my own devices
Never was I safe
no not even then
but we didn't know such
things then
at least not like we do now

But those were the days
of no instant communication
where I could memorize
at least a dozen phone numbers
But then there were
no cell phones and no internet
no 24/7 fear-porn media
This, this hadn't caught up to us yet

So child in me, child of then
Do I offer you candy now?
And please, for the love of God
just say no

Hole in one

I'm so bored said the boy
to his aloof friend
What kind of trouble
can we get ourselves into
today… said the boy

And the many long hot days
brought us to be
so stupid, so reckless
and yet somehow creative

How many times did it happen
where we got expelled
from a golf course
running through or riding our bikes
in the path of a well-placed sprinkler
But the best part was
how hard the water hit us
the water pressure knocking you down
This was the pure joy of our stupidity

I have yet to figure out
if it's my own idiocracy
or my persistent boredom
that's a gift to my adulthood
One thing I do realize however
is that it is the seed
of my creativity

Growing up in the 80's

Growing up, we had cheap cars
Chevettes, Pintos, and Beetles too

Growing up, we were middle class kids
I wore clothes handed down
from my brother and cousins too

Growing up, I chewed a lot of gum
blew a bubble so big
it got stuck in my hair
Mother was less than pleased

Growing up, we used to play with matches
that's back when lots of people smoked
we'd just walk into any store
grab a book and walk out
just like nothing

Growing up, we built a lot of plastic models
then used the matches to set them on fire
Our dad was the Fire Chief

Growing up...
we got in trouble a lot
the rest is history

Fornicator

A man is so weak
as he lives by the instinct
and so driven by one's own
flesh and blood
a hollow desire

Here I lie, here I do wake
as I will live, so shall I die
I am so weak, for it is in you
that I lust for, living by
the breast and by the thigh

The curvature of your spine
where my lips grow hungry
Kisses I do give to you there
the flesh of your lower back

With eyes closed I see,
A red flower in the tall white grass
hidden beneath the sheath of night
where my lost hand holds onto you
beneath the impulse of blood
on a harvest moon

First Kiss

Did you say you wanted,
wanted to hold hands?
At first glance
it was awkward
the first kiss

There are some things in life
that can be terrifying
like your first kiss

And there are some things in life
that are truly awkward
like your first kiss

Caught in the moment
the back seat of a car
you gave me your
first kiss

Today, I had a far off memory
and it was
of a first kiss

Father Time

And it was in her kitchen
that was to be
a cramped space,
dust hanging in the light
Belonging to my old grandmother
hanging there, made from white pine
moving in its rhythm, a simple clock

Quite often, I spent my winters there
Cold days, where I was left alone
to play in solitude
In fits of boredom,
clumsily digging through rusty trinkets
The memories of their life
from the post-war days

With my eyes now closed so tight
I can see it...
balls of yarn, sewing needles and
old pocket knives
These little things, they were
treasure to me. I often looked them over
each time hoping to perhaps
find something new
maybe even
something unclaimed by time

Whisper Head

This gray house now sits vacant
on a busy street
In it, is your memory
perhaps something old fashioned
maybe a little something left behind
that sits outside of time
outside of my memory
a little piece of you
that holds me so dear
a child

I once played there
in this old house of yours
this grandchild of yours,
the now loving memory
of mine

There, a memory of dark oak floors
with little toy cars and airplanes
with the quiet soft ticking
of your old clock
counting away the minutes

And now there it rests
high upon its wall
reminding me of the days
that I thought would never end
softly, so softly ticking
there it was
just in time

Drinking

The hour is dark,
as people will fade
into the shadows
So, is it time for whiskey
and is it time for beer?

Our ships are about to
get wrecked, so you'd
better steer clear
rough seas ahead
go forlorn

Later that night
we can all stagger home,
as sheets caught to the wind

When the dawn comes again,
the dew moistens the grass
of an early spring day
Our skulls will all be
broken, there upon
the rocks, alone
and broken

Dearest Daughter

My dearest daughter,
I can see so clearly now
that you are a reflection
of me

To this I say
I can also see through
your eyes
as I too have walked
this Earth

To all things, I say
glorious victory
Both you and I share
the basic DNA

But you, as an old soul
must once again agree
to see my life as something
more than who I really am
ssshhhh it's a secret...

A father, yes, I am
but you are as I, as in One
my daughter
Be who you are! I say
Be glorious! I say
and always be happy,
I say

And perhaps someday
you shall look upon my words
my words at play
and see, see just who I am
as I write for you
to see me
as a simple man
who I really am

Child's Play

I am in the day of Pan
walking with my hackles up
for all to see

The time of child's play
is far from over for me

I toss the ball to you
from behind me
as the sun catches
your eyes

Feel the dirt of the Earth
beneath your bare feet
as we play
back and forth
and then there we were

Do you even dare to believe,
that we are eternally young
all at once and there we are

The child of the heart,
suckling at the mother's
warm breast
and here we are
together, as one warm breath,
children of the olde Earth
both eternally

Buying Candy

We both had paper-routes that summer
It was boring that summer too,
long hot and boring

As boys we could leave
and not come home until
much much later
after sunset

With our bicycles
we were free to go
just about anywhere
we damn well pleased

Some days were fun
jumping off the waterfall
down at the Muddy River
where we hid the dirty magazines
we had found just beyond
your neighbor's yard
and what did we know about sex
anyway?

The world I live in today
isn't the same, not at all
Kids are all medicated
they don't come outside
and I don't see their bicycles
outside the local 7-Eleven

Dear children,
technology it seems
has killed your childhood memories

Boys on Bicycles

I could have wasted by younger years
There were times of course
when I fell and scraped my knees
and ran off into the woods getting lost...
I even fell out of a tree once
where a pile of leaves saved me

There were many many times
that I've fallen, it's true
And then it was
from bicycles, skateboards, and rocky cliffs
But the worst was falling from love
and what would life be
without your first kiss?

Yes, I could have wasted my younger years
I too, cried my tears like anyone else
and felt the endless boredom
of summer days

Looking back now,
I truly know, I know nothing was wasted
In my innocence, I had such strength
I could have wasted my younger years

Bad choices

When you are so young
let it be said
that there are no bad ideas
and if it weren't for my own stupidity
I wouldn't be so smart today
my only regret is
not having,
not having that same fearless stupidity
for life ain't worth living
if it is filled with fear

A lovers breast

I know where the night sings
It is in your arms
it is at your breast
it is next to your cheek
the warmth and texture
of skin next to the night

How on earth I know such things
is not for you to believe
but instead, it is for me to know
yes in all my truth

I know why it is that I love
I know there is an emptiness
that resides within my heart
a place of the empty heart

and it is you, you who took
the risk, the risk to love me
for it is you who are at fault
here, yes, most certainly
it is you

Now, do open hearts sing
or do they cry? Do real
thoughts of honesty
just happen, like those
who suddenly have opened
up their eyes to see truth?
I think not, no it is my truth
to love someone by accident
by shear happenstance
yes, that is love's truth

A fallowed field

There is this place
 where I used to walk
A field adjacent to the farm
 sometimes filled with cows
sometimes used to grow corn
 and even an occasional hunter
or two trying to catch pheasant

The only landmark was an elderly oak tree
 standing alone, looking down at me
where there was a short foothill
 I used to love to go there
all by myself, sometimes with a friend
 A field, with its blades of golden grass

This was my private constellation
 the place I first asked the question
Both whom and what were you, God
 and why was I left here all alone
That's where I was in my mind on that day
 all alone with my thoughts
on your warm summer day
 just thinking of you

A boring summer

It was in the innocence of my boyhood
that I saw you
not on purpose of course
No, it was quite by accident
as some things are very innocent

There was me on my bike
and you in your kitchen window
standing there naked
for all who came past
to see

Me, just rolling on past
nothing better to do
nowhere in particular to be
that day, just riding my bike

He was your man, that I did see
in your house of majesty
it wasn't my place
but I did see...

Just rolling on past
totally bored
but now with a
good summer's memory

Boys of a certain age

During a certain age
we as boys, were wild and free
staying out late
making all manner of noise
beneath the street lights
Our shadows were yet to be men

On my bike, I'd come home
in the dark, chased by shadows
and did my parents even care?
We stayed out too late
and with not much of a care

Some nights, I'd have a friend sleep over
and we'd wander out into the night
late after the hour of dark
The occasional car would pass us by
so we would yell out, Ditch!

As the game went
you couldn't hesitate
no matter where you stood
you would have to jump
for the nearest brush or bush
and boy I hated the prickers

Whisper Head

When I was your age, daughter
I would stay out too late
hiding and playing
into the black of night
yes, when I was your age

ACT 2.
Winter

We are called brothers

I feel your exclusion
but didn't understand it
Were you lost somehow
or maybe even forgotten
brother of mine?

Oh brother of mine
you do live where
tears aren't welcome
the house of a stone heart
haunted by compassion

Is this where you were brought to?
The house of a monster
the place of the heartless witch
where shadows of love run from the light

and when did you decide
that it was all to be given up?
What brought you to that point
of not speaking to me?

Am I here to be your truth
Do I reflect your truth
and is it your own reflection
that sends you so far away
from me?

That day, I was there
the day they told you
that you didn't look like me
and it is why, you can't...
You can't speak to me
Trailing pain,
it does haunt you
I can so surely see

Here I am,
we are called brothers
don't let it stop me
from being your truth

The hurt closet

If you want to say something
then let it be heard
all around...
But no, she had a frozen heart
A heart, too filled with, your hurt
haunted by a mother's ghost

A fatherless child, who grew up
in the shadows of a loveless marriage
born to cocaine and alcohol
addiction

Some people never leave
the shadows of their past behind
Living with all parts detached
like little pieces of paper
blowing around and through
their vacant lives

The door was right in front of you
only you chose to ignore its effigy
Behind the door, sitting in the dark
is your light, only you
and only you can pull its string
as it leads to your heart
The place, that you hide your hurt

That door now sits in your past
It waits in a vacant house
on a forgotten street
where no one will ever live
on this dead end street

Long forgotten was her door
and so cold grows the heart now
Only thing we can see
is the soft florescent sign
that flashes *vacancy*

Syndrome

Growing up, my mother was a drunk
it bothered me
the raw stillness
the simple lack of understanding
by me

First it was her and then it was him
Someone please hold me,
and who's my parent today?

My first breath came in vain
under the vise she lived with
a blue-eyed boy
so fetal, so harmed
and maybe even sick

I live in a world today
where laws serve
to govern man
But none do protect
against the crime
my mother was to commit
unto me

Sledding

Cold winter shoes
meet with cold winter feet
Together as young boys do
we walk to the biggest hill
to show it, its defeat

No sooner do we yield
to the bitter cold
and a retreating sun

Frozen faces and
cold winter hands
Home we all trudge
where a warm hearth awaits

One last breath

Every day they are reporting
to the cases of life and death
The map I see is growing
into a darker shade of red
Both the fear and contagion
are now spreading

My body is only a shell
a lowly husk to carry my spirit
the eternal spark, that which is
the All Father

If this infection should take me
to where my vessel is nil,
I know that life is my death
and death is my life

And it is when I draw a final
breath, as you're standing over me
that my spirit will once again
sing and ride free

Why is it, we cling so closely to life
when it is in fact death
that sets us free

At my age, an average middle aged man
I've seen my fair share of people expire
Each time, it is with a hidden anticipation too

For I do want to know,
and are you free now? Is the Holy Spirit
shining deep within you?
Is the world to now be seen
through a rose colored glass?
And is the end, really just the beginning?

Old wounds

And I looked
and I looked
and I looked...

Just until, I thought I could see
you. Though it was brief
and I was a naive child
not quite yet a man

Still then, it did hurt me
when one day, you just decided
to say no. No to me?
I was dust, swept off
and away, set adrift
to the hollow ocean, of blue
than red, then green again

Until one day it was my turn
to break someone else's heart
I had to know, I had to see
Did it feel so bad
like it did to be the receiver
of bad and unwanted news

Let me tell you that
today, and today, until today
you are no longer
my lover, I am setting you free
adrift to the ocean
of your own imagination

When I was John

It's time to walk in the snow again
He said this looking down at me
as smoke from a pipe
hid his foolish grin
and the sun was parting the trees
on that day

This was a man who grew up
knowing things I may never have to
The things you might know
when you only have a few quarters and a nickel
to your name

This man of old recanted stories to me
of the watercress, elderberry, planting tomatoes
and the saving of seeds
I always thought how lucky he must be
to know the ways of old
to have seen things and had struggles
that I will not know

And what must it take
to be a man of old
to have such wisdom
and such strength
as I simply stood there
in his shadow

A formidable man in his time
I am so sure
But as for today, he was blocking the sun
so that I may see
into the wisdom of his shadow

Her choice

If I am an echo of my past
does it mean that I've fallen
from grace

Having fallen so hard,
flat on my face, hitting the Earth
blood being spilled, on that day
Awakening to a new reality
a bad dream, the murky bottom

I've lost all trust at this point
but if you returned to me
just to remind me of then
that very moment
where I cried
and so did you
it will all be too much
for me

We were so young
wisdom hadn't touched us yet
two children in the darkness
one touch

Whisper Head

It wasn't yours to keep,
was it? And then I just fell
I'm sure that it hurt you
as it hurt me too

The echoes of my past
do haunt me sometimes
and
you are there, to tell me
again and again and again
but no one,
no one is to blame
as I hit bottom
a fleeting glimpse of pain
the simple truth

Hell if it's me

I hold my mistakes
and for you to not notice
is near impossible

It would have been easier
if I was just made of stone

But now, now I'm digging deeper
Too many lies have been told
too many to know what's real for me

This reality, this time frame
is it even real for us?
Are we a family anyway?
Three kids, two families
two of everything

Does the world just collapse
in on all of us?

Whisper Head

The water flows like truth
washing over me
like I was just made of stone
solid in a frozen state
Lost in a place I can not be
submerged in the confluence of me

One day I'll wake up
and it won't be me anymore
as I had been washed away
into the tides of emotions

Then I suddenly woke up
gasping for air
and then I realized
it was nothing but truth

Go be sad

I want you to be sad
but not because of us
or what was ever lost
No, it is for revenge
as I sink my teeth
into the words that
once hurt me, as I
hurt you in turn
Spilling my sorrow
as tears do fall
to my dirty feet.

Don't break my heart

Both eyes are blind
to how the mind changes
over such lengths in time
In the same way that my eyes
are blind to how we've aged
together

Aged? We are now getting,
a little older
Lets say only halfway
but I, as in me
feels the changes
to come

Some days it is
my aches, my pains
Tomorrow it may be
my heart
For if you are taken
from me, too soon
I'm so sure
it will all start to hurt
me

But for now, this moment
I breath as I live
and some day, I too
will die

Dear Wife

My wife, I will cry for you
if you will only cry for me

I am lost for you
if you are lost within me

The things I love about you
I only hope, you can love about me

I am only human, naked
and then too
almost always
I am lost in my thoughts
so please forgive me

Can you forgive my offense?

You are the very best mother
to our only daughter
our only child,
Yes, that I can see

No other parent do I know
that has such devotion
and such honesty
so thoughtful
and devoted
too

Whisper Head

I know, if I am at all honest
that you are much better
than me, than I,
yes me

No, it's not to cast insult
upon myself
no
it's to acknowledge
the hard work you have done
What has been given here

And who else would ever know
where my socks are
where I left my keys
what dessert I want made
how I like my coffee
the best way, to fold my shirt
and keeps track
of all our paperwork
and pays the bills on Wednesdays
who else, but you
my wife

Can't touch

You can't hide a ghost
in your tree

There is something,
something that's haunted me
since you've known me
as a boy,
still yet to be a man

It isn't nice and no
it isn't pleasant
definitely not fair
either

But you should know
that there is something
that has haunted me

In darkened places
the recesses of my mind
the place I hid before you
the place, he can not get to me
No, you will never touch me
again

Broken child

I just stood there
an innocent child
before you
and then I just wept
standing there and then
I told you of my pain
and suffering
my grief

But then there was you
my father, the fallen
How could you?
How could you not even
hold me? Are you that way,
so broken that you posses
none of this thing
we call empathy
how could you
father to a child
in me

And there I stood
but you couldn't even
not ever, just hold me
As I hurt, yes, I am in pain
it's me you see
your child

Boy is a man

What if, I'm a ghost to my past
a person whom I once was
to be, one you can no longer see
or recognize

If a boy stands before you
I, as in me
please know that he was once a man
too

Look deep into his eyes
and see the reflection of pain
for we do not get through this life
without first scraping our knees
At least that is what I think
that I believe

For today however, I stand before you
to show you evidence of my bare hands
as proof, that I've somehow grown up
to be the man within the boy within the man
But am still so innocent, as here I stand
I, as in me, into you

Black and white faces

There are children who call to the north
and their voices are wanting to be heard
How far have they traveled to sing these words
How often do they feign grief as you look away
I am still at a crossroads now, even to this day
the sun it sets, past and parted there are those
who simply look away. They look away.

Amish Shaker

This day, we do arrive in the old house
lost to a place frozen in time
and from across the room I do see
dust floating through the air
just as it catches the sunlight

The dust of a hundred years fallen
telling the story that time forgot
So surely it was breathed in by
the many generations of
farming families here,
the salt of the earth people

What of the dust anyway?
this old dirt that clung,
it clung to the air
and did it escape from
their lungs or a whisper
from their last breath
And did the dust contain
any of their tears?

This old house, on a day
close to the eve of an autumn day
The red, yellow and brown
cupping leaves haven't yielded
to the coming cold snap
No, not quite yet

Whisper Head

A cold chill runs down my neck
and I can almost see her
The stern yet elegant farmer's wife
A pure white apron, putting out
a freshly baked apple pie
And do I smell this in the dust,
and a hint of cinnamon too?

What is lost is never forgotten
as the footprints of time are
always haunting to me

A home to man

One solitary footstep
lands upon the earth below me
Just like one solitary footstep
lends hope for a new direction
for all of mankind on this day

It is on this day that humanity
will most certainly awaken
And it is in the awakening
that they so surely will realize
the error in their ways

Spaceship Mother Earth, Gaia
she is mother to all her children
The humans, ants, bees, birds
and farm animals alike

So it goes for the animals
as so it goes for the humans alike
If you should sow ugliness and hatred
so shall you breathe it into your life
and if you show her love and respect
so shall you be allowed to till the fields
and reap the bounties of plenitude

A finite balance must be kept here
for nothing is forever, nothing
is infinite on the planet we call Earth
If you love it, so shall it love you back
As a mother never forgets her children

A Couple

If I open a box in winter
will you be there?
If I lie in a bed of leaves in autumn
will you die with me there?
And if I sing a song off key
will you sing louder, so that
I may not be heard?

At times in our lives
it is difficult to know who
exactly we are…
Sometimes we can get lost
in our thoughts, in our emotions,
and in our wanting

Tomorrow is another day for us
but we still have today
and that is where we live,
in today, let's just have that

A bird song

I hide from your words
oh, how they haunt me
and I hide from myself
so what else can I do?

There are two versions of me
like there are two versions of you
My face meets yours
in the darkness of your pillow

We need not be truthful
as love haunts us like a memory
and we take its whispers
and its aspirations
then hold them so closely
bearing witness, to our hearts

So hold me when you need love
as I pull you into my being
then birds will come,
as the seasons change throughout you
singing songs of reason
for the coming of rain

ACT 3.

Fire & ice

In the way of things

Standing there up on top of a high ridge
looking out, deep into the forest of the Fey
a very light snow can be seen, as it is just
starting to paint the canvas of earth below.

The singularity exists in each and every tree here
Each of the ancient pine contains its own spirit,
as each of the ancient conifers carries its own seed
The lowly pine cone, an ability to replicate
both into the unity and oneness alike.

Much in the same fashion that the big bang started it all,
only now, time is getting older, it is moving on from itself
That lowly pine cone shudders, then drops to the earth
searching both for its death and resurrection.

From the high ridge, off in the distance, nature's breath blows
ever so slowly, this breath of life comes across the land
like a whisper, it falls upon a grey ground squirrel
in a perfect synchronicity, the squirrel hears the Word,
a message about what she must do.

Sweeping out across the land, both Nature and squirrel become one
They are a complete singularity, being one, and being the many
She picks up the pine cone, clutching it in her teeth
then once things are in alignment, the right spot is found
hidden in the unseen vortex within a circle of rock
among the frozen moss in the shadow of an oak
The pine cone is brought unto the earth once more.

In the tradition of time immortal, life begins and so it dies
The sun rises and then it sets, as it follows the seasons
From the fallen leaves and bark, from the old moss,
and from the remains of life, only fertile ground remains.

And in that silt, life is being renewed, and it is in the darkness that
a life giving seed emerges once again, reborn in unity and oneness
in the vortex, and into the circle of rocks, a new ceremony emerges
The Fey have all gathered there, to see as the grandfather pine cone
becomes the pine tree, the one who was foretold to be grand,
to be the tallest in the deep woods, and even while next to a master oak
All the trees know that their bows must break to give sun to the son.

Once more the seasons must change, once more the encroachment
of man threatens the deep woods of Fey. Off in the distance, houses
emerge and generations of men do pass, they stop, they start, they repeat
And in the span of some ninety years, the master pine tree emerges
It emerges! to both the sun and the clouds, as if to say God, I am here!

Just in a matter of time, men have started to hunt in the forest and have
also started to gather wood and sometimes they are tricked by the
Fey, getting lost all day walking in circles, deep through the thickets,
boots stuck in the mud, tools lost or the occasional
acorn hits them in the head. What is brought to the forest,
belongs to the forest, and as they say, it shall be.

In the mornings of Spring, the Fey have started to invite children into
the deep forest where the breath of life can be felt and the imagination
can run wild and free, unencumbered by the lies of men.

On this particular day of Spring, it is to be the most special of days,
it is the day that the yellow daisies and daffodils will sing, all while
drawing in the children at play, playing games of hide and seek
But only today, there is to be a lost boy, one who is left behind
He is left alone and afraid in tears of dirt sitting beneath the
Great Pine Tree. The tree that connects the heaven and earth.

As the sun reached its peak at a time around noon, the pine
tree speaks to the boy, and as he looks around, he inquires
Who's there? It is me, the eldest of the pines the father
to the oaks, a home to the Fey. Follow my voice it says
to the boy, follow it and I'll set you free. The boy says,
but I am free! No, the pine argues back, you live in a
prison, confines of which you can not see...

The boy stands up and shouts, shut up, I am too free!
Oh, are you the pine says in rebuttal. Yes, in fact I am.
The pine pokes back one last time, if you wish to know
what it is to really be free, you must climb me, you must
climb me from the cool moist earth to where the sun
kisses your face.

Now the Great Pine stood ready and prepared for this day
It had grown the most perfect of branches to be climbed
like both ladder and stair. Each bow was held both proud
and strong. All the other trees remember, had moved
aside for the Great Pine. It touched both the Heaven and
the Earth.

Slowly the boy approached the tree, slowly the boy gripped
the first branch, and slowly the boy ascended the ladder
of the Great Pine Tree. All the way to the top, all the way there,
minutes turned into hours, hours turned into days, days into weeks
and weeks into years. Slowly, every so slowly he climbed
the Great Pine Tree.

As the boy broke through to the sky, he emerged as a man
A man who had been weathered by time, and as a man who took
in all the wisdom he could ever see, for it was the Great Pine who
imbued this knowledge to him you see.

The man who was the boy who was the man could see far
and wide across the land and he could see the world had
changed. The town had become a city, the sky had become
dirty and he could no longer hear the flowers singing.

Looking, staring and longing for his boyhood, the man
could so clearly see. He could see the hand-print of man
and it made his heart hurt, it made his mind break,
and it made him long for the innocence of his youth.

The Great Pine spoke so softly and with compassion
to the boy who was a man who was a boy. Listen, I
have one last thing to show you. Yes, said the man?
You have to learn what faith is now, and that means
to trust what you can't see and what you can not touch.
And how is it I do that, he replied? You must now climb
past me into the nothingness of the sky. But why said the man?
Because I have brought you all the way to the edge of Heaven,
to the Father of all creation. Whose father? replied the man.
The Great Pine whispered, the All Father.

After all these years and after all this time, aren't you my father?
No! replied the Great Pine. You must understand that everything
is One, so in course there is no end and there is no beginning. So
I give you one last lesson, this one last test. You must see into the
nothing, look through that which is your heart, and forgive all
that is your hurt. The man finally relents, takes a deep breath, climbing a
little further until he can climb no further. The man says, so now what?
Further, go further, and then the man moves further and reaches for
the nothing, climbing into the emptiness of time, the emptiness of space
and in a sudden flash of light, in the matter of an instant, he is turned to light.
The boy who was the man who was the boy had gone to be part of the
Oneness

Spear of destiny

1.)
The ghosts of our past
are hidden under our feet
as there they are in the dry hot sands,
where there is an arid parched earth
In such a time of early Spring
herders of goats and sheep alike
were seen from a distance
on a far off ridge, during
a sunrise, as we did mourn.

As the All Father commanded
a blood moon had appeared on
the eve of his crucifixion
It was during that night
that we sat and prayed for him
and before us he did appear...
How, we could not understand,
in a bright spirit, walking in no mortal
body, he did give to us his last message
before he took to a physical death.

"Look at this body, as it exists
between our Heaven and Earth now.
It is not yours to return to the grave,
as it has always existed to and for the
Father of all creation. No mortal shall steal
these words, for they are mine, and
mine alone. Let it be then said, here
and now, all mankind shall walk this way,

towards the light, towards a oneness,
towards a unity with each other."

As quickly as he came, so did he leave.
Leaving us to our own thoughts
and what of this oneness and unity?
How are we to spread his words?
Shall we write them? Or shall we
forever tread upon this earthly estate
casting out these words like seeds
to be sewn, so they may be born again?

2.)
There, now, it was to happen, and there
we silently stood, all thirteen of us, both
men and women alike, both as equals
A unity in his words had bonded us
throughout this space and time
This circular event that was soon,
was so soon to transpire.

From a distance we could see him,
falling to his knees, being whipped
by the most wicked of men, the
kind of men who had serpents blood in
their veins, the soils of the serpent,
It lived in these kind of men, a blood
line of those who were cast out, a
blood line of those who were fallen,
and a blood line that enslaves. Even
then we knew better, as the All Seeing
Eye was to be a shadow upon us.

And as they grew closer still, to
us, standing on the mound, I could
hear the foul words and smell their stinking
breath. I spoke to the twelve, I said to them
"Men, let a woman's voice be heard here
and today, a new morning will come,
let this event never be forgotten. Today
we will see his blood being spilled
as he was chosen and has chosen in
his own freewill. So shall he be sacrificed,
in the name of all greatness, and all
that is good."

As the words left my mouth, the twelve
turned their backs to me, silently they
stood there, waiting, waiting for the
foul creatures to come closer still. Then
they did come, with the son of man, his body
so sadly ripped and torn by their cruelty.
One of the men whispered, daring not to
shout, and what will come of this? How
is it we will return to our lives after this!
How can this foul and awful thing be
allowed by our creator? No man or
women dared to speak up...

With whips, chains, and spears,
we could see from afar. The men
took aim upon him with a hammer and
nail, one after another, after another
as he did scream for the All Father,
he did, I heard him plead for his life.
Ever so slowly did they raise his cross,
with its effigy of blood soaked wood.

3.)
My Angel said to me:
"Now, all rise, all rise, here me sing"
The distant voice faded away to black
only faint cries of whispers were being heard
Tears ran down my face, and as they ran down
my face, I could only continue to cry until
I cried no more.

As I wiped the tears from my eyes, I could
discern no more, pieces of me now lay
broken upon the floor. Never shall it truly
be understood, as to why such a sacrifice
had to be given?

The Angel says to me once more:
"Now, all rise, all rise, all rise"
I'm suddenly called back to my life,
my life in the here and now,
as I draw in the deepest of breaths
both awake and aware, a stranger to here,
a stranger from far off time, a far off place.

The Angel commands me:
"Now, all rise, all rise, it is time to be reborn"
So clearly I could remember his effigy,
the wooden cross, the crown of thorns,
as my heart stood still, and yet it pounded
So clearly I do remember, the time of before
the star was taken from us.

He speaks once more:
"Now, all rise, all rise, today you are a man,
reborn unto a time you will barely understand,
into a state of being filled with tribulations,
with thoughts of him, and thoughts of self,
which now fade into your memory."

I rise, as I rose to be here today, A lost
disciple, A lost soul, A key holder
of the kingdom to come that we were so promised,
A humble vessel who hath to bring new words
Oh, a day of rebirth of the son of man awaits me.

Looking into the mirror I can see him,
as I do see myself. Looking at these two hands
I see him within me, we reside together
into the spirit of man, the spirit of One, amen.

The Antediluvian

1.)
It was on the seventh day
of the seventh hour
on the seventh Earth
that the Antediluvian appeared
for the very first time, out of nowhere
dressed in black desert garb, which shielded
him from the piercing heat and the blowing sands.

He was to be the man, the very last man
who could possibly stop the Dark Star
an advanced form of A.I. that had infected
all of the Earth's within the parallel universes,
The Dark Star had systematically collapsed
all of them into a black hole, into a nothing.

This entity, this machine, this ecosystem
had deployed itself like a virus
A virus that could not be detected, as it
was truly symbiotic even with our own human
flesh and blood.

The Antediluvian, the last man, the last Hebrew
carried with him the word of One. On the seventh
Earth, like in all things the virus had hijacked that
belief system too. But he, the one, had in his
possession, the last book of One, the truth.

Again, maybe it was divine timing...
but just in time, this one last man walked out
of the dry scorched desert and into the dimensional
reality of seventh Earth. He was to be the last
survivor, with the last book, that contained
the final words and memories of Oneness.

Know this now:
All of the worlds of Earth had collapsed into one another,
one smashing the next and the next and the next,
until a great nothing appeared
The virus was to consume even its own self
It lusted after everything that the son of Adam had
ever created, every footprint, and every written word.

And it ate like a cancer does eat
No more history, no more happy families,
no more Sundays of worship, no more
children at play, no more holidays, no more
unity, and no more equality.

And how is it that we knew that it was here?
How do we see it on the seventh Earth
on the seventh day of the seventh hour?
You must look for its mark, look for
its sign, and look for its influence
in all things human.

You will see it like a cancer spreading.
Everywhere it will divide and it will
conquer, it will cause great divisions:
There will be rich vs. poor
There will be black vs. white
There will God vs. Church
There will be destruction of unborn life

There will be pollution that poisons you
There will be lines in the skies
There will be stealing and looting
There will be greed and starvation

Then there will be its enslavement
of humanity and its humanness
A black box will be placed at the
base of your necks. It is called
Trans-humanism. Man and
machine will become one. It shall
bear the mark of the Black Star.

2.)
It is important to know just when it was
that he did arrive for us. And there we
were, standing amongst the trees, in the
last forest, 46.2276° N, 2.2137° E
The smog and poisons of the machines
had killed everything else, everything
else but the small island we stood upon there.
The seventh Earth, on the seventh hour,
of the seventh day.

The Antediluvian did appear to us
as a stranger from a strange land,
speaking a tongue that had not been
spoken since the time before the
great flood. And it was the flood
that had wiped out the virus for
us then, only now in this time we
were so far from the One.

-A lost tribe, a lost people,
the last humans who still believed,
who still believed in One.

3.)
The desert man slowly approached
these lost souls of the seventh earth
The elder of the group stepped forward
from amongst them to translate his message.

He shared his story about how his world
had collapsed under the weight of the
Black Star, and that it had eaten its fill.
A great story he told that was hard to describe
and hard to believe, to be excepted in good faith.
"I am the last man, the last Hebrew,
the last priest who has been brought
to you as I carry the word of One,
and so it is that I shall teach you of this."

For weeks, months and years he started
to teach the last tribe as he had promised
his people he would do, as they were the
very last hope, the very last tribe, the
very last people to speak the words
of oneness and unity. His words would
bring them to the only way of escaping
this last habitat on this last earth, and
that road to hope was to be called ascension.

To the desert man's last remaining breath
he had taught his new tribe the secret,
and that was that we were all One, and if
you were to transcend this world of suffering,
you needed to go inwards, deep into the soul
of the self. You see, once you realize that
you are creator itself you are no longer separate,
you are no longer divided, you are no longer lost,
you are no longer enslaved, and nothing can truly
kill or harm you, as you are all an infinite oneness.
Once you know that, you will never cease to exist.

When at war

Night Angel, night Angel
can you please protect us?
Protect us from our pains
as we do pray for protection
during these times of crises.

Yes, the crises, the bombs, the death
and the screams, yes the screams!
Hold on tight, our most heavenly
Angels, as we call for you by night,
as the bombs drop all around us.

God, do send us your bravest Angels,
most importunately during these
uncertain times. And it is man's will
to do harm to one another again.
How lost they are too!

Will you come to us Angels?
Will you please remember us?
Will you come by night as we pray?
We ask of you to please save us.

The Prophecy

There, the Angel did come for me
I was swept up and away with him
So surely, it was during the dark of night
Softly, very softly, we floated away
into the sky of night.

As we glided gently through the air
I did hear chaos ring true. And there
I did ask him, what of this?
How have I been fooled,
into being taken somewhere
not deemed safe by our creator?

He stopped, held me still, as I floated
over the Earth on that night, and night
was turned into day. Looking below
us, so high at the edge of heaven
we did float. The ground beneath
us erupted into a fire. It was the desert floor,
with houses, lost sand, bright lights and
gambling machines stained by mortal addictions.

All of a sudden the Earth became unzipped
and she bled, as if being wounded by
the Creator himself. A strong and powerful
voice shook me through and through,
"Behold, the sinners shall be taken back
unto the Earth." There, I took witness
to the tragedy as it unfolded.

It seemed to go on forever and I shook
with a dramatic fear. There I could see,
it went all the way out to the ocean,
and it went all the way out to the sea.
In this day we do end, and silently the
Angel is still watching over me.

The last nail

I cannot raise the dead
like you can
I cannot heal the lepers
like you can
I cannot bring the prophesy
like you can
and I cannot bless those that need
like you can

If they were to gather before me,
gather with me here right now
How could I ever begin
to tell your story,
without first explaining your death
the great redeemer of our sins

What would I even say?
I know that I saw your end
I too was there, but is that all
I really know? I think not

It is my burden to remember
as it is my burden to forget
I heard it, as I saw it
the rust covered iron
when they drove the last nail

The Father

There he stood
a man before God
the All Father

and then in a moment
of passion and gratitude
he drops to his knees

Tears are now running from his eyes
blood, it bleeds from his hands
and asking for mercy
the day he is to be
reborn
as the son of man

Striped Pajamas

My words are soaked in blood
and the guilty have run to the fence
They stand and stare at me
the innocent one, in stripes

The star is shown on my coat
A badge of honor, one of frailty
and one to show, that we are
all God's chosen people
in the land of milk and honey
as we do so deserve

They were misled men
and I do forgive them:
for their brutality
for their savagery
for their vulgarity
for their darkness,
as they are far from God's reach
and even though they walk in
the hour of day, they know nothing
of the light, and nothing of love
For if the heavenly Father is with you,
then you would not be so inexplicably evil

All the limbs now hang from trees
It is at the very edge of dawn too,
where the snow has started to fall
Only here, it is never white

Whisper Head

We stood there with frozen hands and feet
looking through the wooden slats of
a rail car, it could move no more
This was to be the place where we would
put our blessed star to rest

And we wept, we wept for them all
The women who were mothers to our children
and the men who were to be our providers
and the elderly, those who were our
wisdom keepers

I stand here now, in the shadow of your day
as a new threat with blood in its teeth
looks upon you, lusting for savagery
It seeks to divide you, to conquer you,
to hold you as a conquest and to brand you
with its prophesied mark

We are here, the souls of the lost Jews,
standing, watching, waiting...
Waiting to see who will win this battle
of David verse Goliath
We do watch with love and concern,
for your history it seems, is doomed to
be repeated.

Once a cross

All glitter is gold in the eyes of man today,
as I watch the father bleed
His blood does fall to the earth
Our sins are awash in blood now
Does his wisdom then come
to a sudden end?
No the daughter of Christ screams!
His daughter was one of the many,
hidden is our truth
hidden is our blood ancestry,
no man shall fallow this field
We are the truth holders of old
the past that is certain
and may the resurrection come
may it come to this day in time
for our All Father.

Lost Identity

As I stand in long lines of people
the man in the distance is calling out
He is calling for change
and change that will ask of you
to step out of the line

We are all standing in line now,
but why? Cold and frozen to the bone
concrete sidewalks in winters city
as the smell of piss and excrement
permeate the air with a backdrop
of white subway tiles
with blind faces shuffling forward

The man calls for the next woman in line
Now is her chance, but no, she still relents
and she walks forward to be stamped,
branded by a bar code, reminiscent
of a past concentration camp,
one that was erased from our history
books, so no one could remember
and no one would step out of line
and no one would speak out
against the oppressor

If history is to be erased by those,
by those who are so easily offended,
then what of us? Are we to all
go belly up and die for one man's
power and greed? Are we now to
succumb to our past mistakes?
Are we to be slaughtered like the lamb
and did not Jacob already warn us?

Are we all not brothers and sisters then?
Does not the same blood run through
you and I alike? I ask you fellow man,
does it?

Hungry at the teeth

The lips on my face remain closed
yet I call for the breath of my throat,
I call to it, as I need all before me
to hear me, to hear me loud and clear
This is now, this is today.

This time, this cycle of human existence,
it is calling for me to speak more truth
for if the truth were lies then so surely
the lies must be truth. As can you hear
the breath, as it rises into the back of
my mouth before it escapes my lips.

As the breath and the air empties my
lungs, so does the truth. Does the
truth arrive upon your ears in pain?
The truth will hurt? Does it hurt the
ears of the ignorant and disdained?

Come, I tell you all now, the truth
was never more painful to hear.
Let me speak to you about fear.
Fear has made you its slave, and
fear has made you my common
bedfellow today. My light, it
shines down upon your truth
if only you could see it, but no
you've been blinded by the fear
of today.

Clear the sleep from your eyes.
You are not bought as a slave
but are most certainly treated
like one. Me familia we are
not, fair travelers we are
not, and good friends we will
never be if you won't wake
from the sleepy brainwash
of a modern slavery.

So wake up now, for all will
want to see. All will want to
know, and once they know
the world will evolve in but
a second. I snap my fingers
and you are awake. Know now,
that you are all One, but first
you must unplug.

A visit to inferno with Metatron

I was taken into that dark place
the place to be called Hell
I had my Angel with me
and as we arrived, it was through
the mouth of a cave into a pool
of sulfur, the head of a mouth
like a small waterfall. Silently
the Angel stood behind me,
so lofty in his presence.

At first, I was only filled with fear
which was shortly abated by a
sharp reassurance from the Angel
who had guided me to this desperate
place they call Hell.

Then looking down at my feet
I could see that they were bare.
With his guidance we did there transcend
unto the lower level of this place
into the area where a pool of sulfur
had collected. It had collected for all
those souls, the souls who chose this place
this place of self inflicted punishment.

Next, he did guide me to the sands of the shore
and there beached upon its burning edge
I did see a body. This soul I can tell you,
with my own two eyes, I did see, was there
laying in anguish, suffering in an endless
pain. No mercy was to be had for this dark
and long forgotten mortal.

I begged my Angel, to please let me know,
please tell me in truth, what brought this
wrath upon this women's soul? There I did
close my eyes, like a picture, I did see her life
filled with drugs, plain as day I did see her
die too, with a needle in her arm, and a smile upon
her face, then I gasped as the Angel removed
his hand from my face.

There and then my Angel spoke to me
"never mind her pain, and never mind
her suffering, for it is not yours, it is
not your burden. It is only for you to
see, and to realize that they are all here
on their own accord. This suffering
is free choice, it is out of free will."

It was in that moment that I really
understood, that we make our own
beds of suffering, we are the one's
who create our own mortal world
of grief. The image was so powerful
that is captured me. There and then
I really understood, yes I truly understood,
what the Angel had meant by
all this being of our own free will.

One figure, one man

I enter the water as a man
and suddenly emerge as the child
naked, alone, and too frail,
pasty white, under weight
lagging in vitality
and then, in a gasp,
there is a death

Time held me under the waters
it held onto me in the deepest blue
into the darkest depth of its current
until I could breathe no more
but I was to see the light
I was to see its all

It is the water of time
that so surely washed it all away
and
all the stains of my past
will be blessed by the hand of you
Oh, Christed figure who does
baptize me, it is your truth
as it is still relevant today

My one hand then does emerge
from the ocean's breast
and I am released into this world
again as,
One who is renewed,
one who is rejoiced
and one who is just in part
one, as I reflect on that day
A summers day of a
setting sun on a man
who embraced The One

Yeshua

I will live in the day
of a life of a year

I am, reborn unto you all now
The door has now opened
to a new possibility

A new dawn will come
as two hands clap
and very soon
become one

ACT 4.

All of our languid dreams

A man out of time

1.)
It was the year that
Christmas came in July
and the birds flew north
instead of south, as
as the sun seemed
to never set

And,
everyone was much too distracted
to even take notice
as their faces were aglow
with the lights from their
tiny screens,
held in their over-washed hands
worn on belts
mounted on wrists
melted into their skin
and all the like

But then there was Charlie,
an uptown man with an
uptown paycheck and
the apartment
to match

Single, rich, and well-bred
and no lady to weigh him
down on his rise to the top
of the world's pyramid

He lived 40 floors up
in uptown Gotham
where there were people
to take care of your
every want
and your every need,
even at 3 a.m.

Money never slept,
working all day
and all night

2.)
Coming slowly down from his
40 floors of affluence
slowly moving down
from his place of prestige
he arrives at the lobby floor

Walking through the foyer
the staff will say hi Charlie
nice suite Charlie
aren't you great Charlie
we pretend to love you Charlie

Whisper Head

He admires himself while walking
past the mirror in the lobby
as the lights seemed to
suddenly dim
and then get very bright
all at once

As soon as his one shiny
black shoe leaves the brass doors
and touches the cold gray concrete
-the world goes silent

There were no honking horns
no bums asking him for change
no doorman kissing his ass
not a single pigeon stood
at his feet

Silence is all it was
nothing, nothing
and more nothing

Silence… but haunted by the
sound of his own breathing

So self-immersed he was,
that he hardly took notice
at first

Slowly, his eyes woke up to
the fact that he was all alone
and soon there after, the panic
set in and
the sweat ran down
his staunch cheekbone

3.)
Both panting and sweating:
looked up, looked down
whistled, called out and
then yelled out

No soul, no person,
No thing that ever was
...not there to reply back

They were all gone
in an instant:

And
the doorman, the banker
the chef, the steward,
along with the mothers,
and the fathers too

Silence and breathing
just silence and breathing

Parched, his mouth went dry
his cheekbones seemed to
pucker just before he was no
longer able to contain the
fear, he doubles over and
vomits, splattering chewed up
scrambled eggs and toast
all over his black over-shined
dress shoes

Not knowing what to do next,
looks down at his watch
and there is no ticking
no movement
and no time
the hands
had disappeared

Flush with fear, Charlie
runs back into the safety
of his most affluent of
apartment buildings and
demands to be helped

Only, no one was there to reply…
all while he is drenched in
sweat, loosens the neck tie,
spins around towards the lobby
mirror to see what a mess
he's become, feeling so vain

Finally:
there he stood, and there he was
There was no reflection
staring back at him, for he
was a man who had run out
of time

4.)
There was a time where
time never existed

Only problem was that
time didn't know that
time never existed

It was only when it was
thought into being
that it somehow
became a real thing

But if it was never thought
than more simply
it never was

and this was only discovered
long after they started
not to believe in it

Part 2:

A nicely dressed man, laid on the marble
floor in his own vomit, covering his ears
and screaming into the void

Still, Charlie could hear nothing. It was
like someone had stuck plugs in his
ears all while his head rang like a car
accident and his reality had been crushed
bumper to bumper

A soft whisper came:
green walls fall on three
green walls fall on three
green walls fall on three

Still, he laid there in a pool of his own bile
the faint smell of pancakes and maple syrup
came across his ruined face, reminding him of
the time when he was five years old, having
a panic fit, being held by his mother

A soft whisper came:
Green walls fall on three Charlie, remember?
Say it with me Charlie, green walls fall on three
It will be okay, the motherly voice said to him

Slowly the man who ran out of time opened his eyes
all while he recited to himself:
Green walls fall on three, green walls fall on three
Slowly, the man who fell apart, then rose to his feet
and slowly turned back to the full length mirror,
checking on his ruined vanity

2.)
Only now, he could see himself once more. Sensing
something else was afoul he looks down to see what
looked liked dirty soapy dishwater running over his
once shiny black shoes

He hears a man's voice now:
Charlie, Mr. Charlie, are you listening now? I have an
important question for you, and I ask it of everyone
that comes through here, the in between space,
the void

What's my question, Charlie asks in anger and humility?
Which one are you? Which of your three reflections
are you?

Are you one, are you two, or are you a three?

Charlie was consumed by the question, knowing
that it was about the summation of his life, as well
as being a puzzle too

The doorman dressed in his burgundy uniform, with
his deep colored smoker's voice, and asks again.
Are you ready to answer Mr. Charlie?

He was still present to the smell of his childhood
breakfast and the faint sound of a motherly voice
and all points were ending here,
and that everything he lived has led to this

What seemed to be an hour, had passed before
Charlie said he was ready to answer the question.
-I'm ready he tells the doorman and my answer
is that I am all three reflections of myself:

I am my past
I am my present
and I am my future
all at once
for everything
is in this present moment

3.)
The doorman speaks in a low drab voice:
You have passed this test, and you are now
free to walk out that door, but with one stipulation.
You shall never assume this life ever again
You will never be Mr. Rich Uptown, 40th floor
and,
you will walk out that door with only the change
in your pocket, and start from the bottom and
work your way back to the top, and you will have
to help others along the way and teach them to
do the same.

The choice of freedom came easy

The turn style door groaned as he pushed and walked
back out to where:
the people came back
the sound returned
his watch turned and ticked
like normal again
but one thing was for sure
nothing, nowhere, nohow
would ever be normal for
him ever again

Old flowers

It is okay, if the past
still haunts you today,
this is what I tell myself
as I am caught off guard
by you again

And yet,
there is blood between us
there is life between us too

I've never known such pain
as when I was with you
and yet,
I am haunted by the scars
not the ones on my skin
but those that are still
underneath it

Never do I have to look
very deep
before I find the pain,
that you had left behind

Today I live for me
today I live for life
and for family
as now I know,
that it isn't what you
can buy or acquire
no, it's what
you leave behind
as your memorial
The breath
of a
life

Not any sense

Are we all just
flesh and blood

what I mean is
are we really real

and don't interrupt me
I'm on a roll

do we say something
do we mean something
and is there purpose
is it all meaningful
and such

I don't really know
and
does anyone really
know

I guess not, because
we're still killing
each other
even right now, at
this very moment
people are killing each
other for no particular
reason, or so it appears
to me

It's all the very same
person, anyway
but
do you see that?

Can I make any sense,
I think not
at least
not right
now
as the moment
has gone empty

Beneath the One Tree

This year,
blood oranges
will come only
in June

And,
this year to the next one
there will be new fruit
at our feet

even as we are:
out of step
out of touch
and maybe
out of time

And as the sun rises
we'll hold each other's
hands while walking
through our orchard

Laughter will be there
and smiles too
along with our long
awaited abundance,
the milk and the honey

And in our orchard,
there is only one tree

That tree will give us:
renewed life
bounty
fertility
imagination
and offspring

And we will all lay there
beneath the One Tree
smelling the air filled
with sweet fruit blossoms

Our children, our offspring
will be able to dance
and they will be able to sing
as they drift off and into a
thoughtful
blissful
imagination
beneath the One Tree

Consummation

The inflamed man
trapped by the wall
of metal
stuck in L.A. traffic
emerges from the car
like a moth from
its chrysalis

He emerges with a
red face, shaved head,
white t-shirt, bad breath
and no companion
to flag him down
or to call him back

The object of his ire
are the
miles of smog puffing
American steel autos

With a cold metal crowbar
in hand
he tries to slay the dragon
with all its flashing red eyes

He thinks he's won
but then he sees another
and another
and then another

Drenched in sweat
completely defeated
he then
drops to his knees

The onlookers don't dare
to shame him
but rather take pity
instead
as they all know too well
that this inferno
of the American dream
gone horribly wrong
is real

Hours later, they all return
to their caves, their dark lives
and watch even more horrors
on the late night news
with a drink in hand
looking for just a little
solace in life

Cow farm

I went to the road
by an island
of a farm
today
so that
the cows could eat
my delicious feet
as I stood
on the fence
built
by the two
hands
of a man
who owns
the dairy farm
that I
wish I
had
today
yes, just me

Dig, dug

Dig, do please dig
as the digger did
dug so deep
that he did
dug much too deep
only now
to dig into the past
and to dig into one's
own future,
for today is only
much too deep

Digger who is to go,
into a fallowed field
to look for the seeds
that he lost in his youth

And he dug into his future
where he did dug too deep
and fell to his knees
and wept
after he did dug too deep

Flesh and blood

As water flows from the faucet
I wash my face as a man

As I am a father to my daughter
so am I a man

Here, I am your husband my wife
I stand for you, a man

and as I shed tears for the loss of
a loved one,
I am still a man
who stands
before God
all alone
as a man

Olde America

You,
you have a wicked son
and a son of a bitch,
he is

Lost in the fields
the slaying fields
that are to be fought over
by the men with long guns

The truth,
it doesn't appear
while they stand in another
man's blood
today

The revolution,
they march and they protest
but don't remember what for?

Spray painted
signs
and
singing birds
bounce to
a new
glory
and
yet

All while our young
men have gathered in
due East fields, where no
birds will lay
as blood drips
from tips of steel
To no good ends
have ever
come
for, or to, here

The youth, too often torn apart
not knowing a direction to take
and no right of passage ever
given to those who are expected
to go out and earn their living,
for the self

The blood lost, lays at their feet
So lost, it was all too much
and a sun set upon
another day
in an olde,
America

Misfortune cookie

I remember,
when there used to be trees here,
do you?

And we were children once,
walking through the high grass
it was up to our arm pits
you could hold your arms out
and pretend you were flying
all while your hands floated up
over the tops of the wheat grass
but then again:

A hurricane would come
a mountain would be moved
a storm would come
an earthquake
a tornado
spilled blood
bullets
all down our alley way
filled with grease traps
broken bottles
old needles
glass pipes
and many other things
of the like

America,
I've come for you today
I hold out my two hands
and I say give me,
give me God damn it!
Please give me
as I ain't got none

A child,
with two broken front teeth
a scraped knee
a broken bike
a deflated ball
model airplanes
scratched records
and
old cassette tapes

And now it's 8:30 a.m.

A white haired woman
says I'm all in,
agreeing to sell what's hers
but this is America
and everything is for sale
both today and tomorrow
and the next
like a fortune cookie
that reads:

"all roads will lead to this"
"seven is your lucky number today"
"don't drink your fucking paycheck"
"play with your kids, while you still can"
"all your neighbors are junkies"

I opt for another cookie, cause they won't
tell me what I want to hear...
not today, not tomorrow,
not never

One nation under

I am the giver of the seed
I am the taker of the seed
as well,
but what am I really?

A father to the world?
I think not
The giver of life?
maybe

A traitor to a nation of thieves?
No, I think not

and what is worse than the sheep,
who have now lined up to march in
an earnest protest, but they
know not what for,
do they?

The birth of this nation is to
come once more
again and again and again,
but what shall it be?!
One of hands fixed in blood?
One that has burned down
each and every effigy?
One that has sworn off its own history?

I turn away in disbelief
I just turn away...

Four legged

I am alone in my mind today
tortured by my own thoughts
making no sense of it
but I have you

I need a companion
until I can be on my own
One who would walk through
hell fire for me
and I found him

I am so simple
but you are so complex
never saying anything
not at all
never a word
but your face speaks
a thousand words

I have this companion
who is my dog
my lowly pit bull
the savior of my
thoughts
mind
spirit
and
my
soul

I know in all of it
at least I have you
today

Second city

I do miss the songs
of my second city

I miss you my Gotham
yes, both today and tomorrow
but just the same
I miss you

And for today
It is just for me,
and for me alone,
yes, it is all
for me

Trapped, I've been delayed
from seeing you again
and
I can't come back to you
for quite some time
No, not just yet

and what of your residence?
They've all been held up
and locked away now
for a good long while
and
perhaps maybe
too long

Soon, yes, very soon
I shall return to you
again
my second city
my Gotham

Get it done

This day,
it has been very long
and empty too
as something is
missing

the clouds will not give
way to the sun
for me

I miss all of its rays
and it is this carpet of clouds
that haunts me
it depresses me
it steals life from me
and
all of my sunshine

The day,
has been chased
by the spitting rain
and you know what?
That is the worst,
either rain, or don't
but don't spit on me
all-day-long

Go forlorn

The wicked shall come
the wicked shall come
go grab your gun

Make your toast while
you still can
and go
have your eggs on ham
as the due sun sits
on today

The wicked are coming
the wicked are coming
go grab your gun

The lights just went out
so we go see by the dark
as the children howl,
into the fear
of night

The wicked are coming
the wicked are coming
so go forlorn

You will stay away,
go stay away
tomorrow is not yet,
to be another day

Lost souls

And what of the dead,
I ask you?

Are they no more,
once given back
to the dirt?

Are they haunted
and tortured
by hearing the
voices of the living?

What of the dead,
I ask you?

Can you hear me now,
bones of the earth?

Our time comes and
it goes like the tides
We all rise and then
will so surely fall

It is our destiny
to lay with the dead
and to only be a
faint memory,
once passed
into the
dirt

Inner conflict

Don't take me apart
if you can't be bothered
to put me back together
again

This time, I mean it

My heart,
it's out on the table
for everyone to see
soft, red and thumping

God knows:
that it's frail and bloody
because sometimes in
life things get messy
These emotions I speak
of can't be locked away
like a bird in a cage
and
we all must sing

Things like emotions are
falling out of my head,
out onto the table now,
There's
numbers, letters and bits
of wood too

And all of this is for you,
can't you see?

Whisper Head

The quiet, the vulnerable
and the meek
the too often, the aging
and the passive winds
at my back, pushing me
towards older yet

And how about you?
We haven't looked at your
heart yet. Let's open it up,
while we are at it
and that head too

The persona is what we all
hide behind:
The dad, the wife, the cousin
the employee, the street sweeper
the garbage man, the business man
a nurse, a homemaker, a cook

One who cares, one who cries, both
the giver and the taker, those with,
and those without, full bellies, and
the starving too

Your feelings are coming tonight
like ghostly bullies wanting to
pick another fight, knocking you
down…

Get up you, God damn it!
Fight to your last breath!

Go see Pop

Hot in July,
the old man
up the dusty road
outside and I
do see him,
at it again

He sits on his front porch
where you can see he is
missing his two front teeth

Time,
didn't care to mention
that all things being here
would eventually
wear out

But he sat and he stayed put
picking his banjo
during the heat of the day
with the sharp sound
of a twang
tap and a bang

And I did say:

Go wave to sweet old Pop
And I said, make sure
he is still with us child,
go yonder
and please see as
I just had this chill,
that ran down my spine,
a feeling that today
might be the day
that the music
finally stops

Green Hell

We were all dressed in green
that day, the day we went to
hell, if hell were green
and
with a humidity that could be
drunk from the sky all while
the bullets flew by our heads,
like a dust
that went up your nose
when the pain got to be
too much
for us

You were sitting in your hooch
that night
and I heard your 45 go off
and I immediately thought the
absolute worst for you
but you said it was only
to kill a rat and then I
handed you a can of
mother fuckers, cause
you looked hungry

Whisper Head

We were in the thick of it,
back to back in the paddy's
and you,
you were my brother
I watched your back
while you squatted in the bush
to take a shit
in the dark of night
while the leeches stuck
to our legs

Yeah, it was a fucking time
one from hell
the green place
where
the heat was up our ass
and after you
kill a man,
your food don't taste right
and
your heart is pretty
much dead at that point
and what was the point,
anyway?

Head of an attic

It is a hot languid day
as I sit and read in the shade
all while a fly is taunting me
-sitting at the rim of my cup
saying to me:
this cold drink is mine
until the death

It is then that I quickly realize,
that there is something dead in me
it's up the stairs, in my attic
the place where all of us hide things,
from ourselves

Yes, I've gone up there quite a
few times over the years
looking through the old records:
people I've known
loves that I've lost
broken dreams
hurt feelings
broken bones
insecurities
and all the like

But as for today
in this searing heat,
it really stinks
to High Heaven
so
I'll have to go up
there again soon

It's only because
the voice is nagging me,
yet again
to go clean shit out
and yes it stinks
and yes it smells
up there
but don't most places
where we hide stuff
that we never want
to look at ever again?

Hearts beating

My heart rests in
an estuary for you
so
please,
please come take
it from me
so
that there
are no more
nights that
are begging
for the
dawn,
so
that our voices
will come to
pass one
another
again
so
that I speak
as if
I've
never spoken
before

My heart
all it does
is wait
for you
as we dream
beside
each other
tonight

In hot water

Hot water,
will become
my next cup
of tea tonight

and it is the string
that holds the
two worlds
together tonight

both the liquid
and the air
making them
speak for
one another
again

it is the string
that will turn
a darker shade
of brown
now, as I wait

and it is the paper
that speaks for the
tea, telling me of
its curse
which needs to
be broken by
the air and
my first sip

steam erupts from
my mug, it meets
the air that fills my
lungs tonight
to where I offer
myself to a
languid sleep

I say to all
goodnight

Just another Jesus

Are you homeless
or are you just truly happy?

I used to pass this beggar
on my way to St. Patrick's
in Gotham city

He would rant and he would
rave, had long hair
like our Anglo Jesus

I did happen, on one occasion
to give him a buck or two

I'm not sure if he was really
homeless or not
but it made no difference
to me

He always managed to
make me smile as I passed
him by

He would rant and he would
rave, having a conversation
only with himself,
no one else

He's the cool kind of homeless guy
that I might like to have dinner
with, but I just bought him a
coffee and danish instead

What was his story?
What are any of their stories?
And who am I to them?

Probably just some rich asshole
passing them by that had what
they didn't, that's all

Two men, too late

A man looks back upon himself
as he lay there dead,
The aftermath of being hit
by a musket ball
the grey was turning blue
and then to a red

All men, some of them boys
gather on the other side
to watch and observe
both the Blue and Grey
to receive them,
no difference
into fields of gold
a land of glory

Listen closely as they speak:

You are not alone brothers
and we are no longer enemies
we all stand here before God
and
we admit to our weakness
and
we admit to our faults,
for we are not being judged
No, not here,
for just being human
if that were to be
our original sin

The shadow of greats

The worker verses the starving writer
in accordance with the deficit of impunity
and all our lives seemed to rollover
some-how, some-where, and in some-way

They stand, all languid, looking at me
and I say to them:

These two hands,
I show you my flesh
as it makes the thin green
money that drives the lives of families
who count on their mouths being feed
by the firmament of a being
who is I

They stand, they say to me,
No but rather now they
must show me that:

Bukowski was a mailman + drunk
Naruda was a communist politician
Whitman was a carpenter with a vision
Frost was a farmer and an honest soul
Dickinson was a sexually frustrated recluse
Hemingway was a macho-man with PTSD
Miller was a hungry pervert who like to fornicate
and then there is I,
a button salesman begging for the scraps
of paper to sell you my words upon

Love of dirt

The farmer,
he has no soul, but
only a thin tap-root
just like
a long white
and black
straw
that drinks up
the life giving earth

He has no more love
for anyone else,
only the dirt:
not his wife
not his son
not his dog
not even
his own daughter

He alone,
is in love with the dirt
and as each season passes
he seduces the Earth
spreading her legs wider
demanding more offspring
at each turning of the
new moon phase

Whisper Head

The farmer,
he is in love with his dirt
So much so, that he marries it
and when he dies
he'll be laid in it,
it's just the farmer
and his betrothed
dirt

R.I.P.

There are no more birds
singing as my father dies
tonight

I am his last legacy now
carrying the burden of
his name's sake
but that is all

And for what
do I carry it
and what of now?
The world we live in,
does it even care?

Pages upon pages
have been written
about this
entanglement
of what is family
and what is blood

I shall go no further now
I've already said enough,
so rest in peace
as I alone will trudge
ahead, to carve
my own path
in Life

Mr. White

He was like no other man
that I had ever met
a man of the sea
a man who toiled
with two hands
building wooden boats
weaving nets
that provided fish
and building pots
that captured bounty
from the oceans floor

No more, he said to me
Walk in my shadow no more

Go learn things, read books
discover people, see yourself
in all things human
sow your oats in fields
that have never been fallowed
lay your head on a rock
by the ocean's tide
and listen to its secrets
listen as you lie
and slowly, you will
become the man
you were always meant
to be

Lust and life

There's a lust in your mouth
as there is a word
upon your lips
that can not be
truly spoken,
at least not tonight

Are you in a fear,
breathing so hard
with a lust for this life
drowning in thoughts
devouring your
own soul

God,
is that a man for you
and your lust?
Go get life,
as it is to be gotten
while falling to
your knees
but only
for the lust
of tonight

Mortician's hours

A full head of greasy
black varnished hair
always dapper
and always clean
but an obsessive clean

Could not, pass a mirror
without checking his
looks

Could not, pass a faucet
without washing his hands

Never would you see him,
in unpressed clothes
greeting them at the door
always dressed in a high collar
shirt; to the nines

After hours:
he liked to smoke a pipe
wearing the classic whore-house
red velvet jacket

He imagined himself separate
from everyone else, was incapable
of feeling love and affection
Paid for it from women
who gathered at the 7-11 store
on East Main Street at midnight

But what he really loved,
is what was so wrong with him
his vile sickness that took place
in the basements of the
mortuaries, after hours

Before he laid out all his tools
and all of his makeup
to make them look like the living
He kissed them
and he kissed them deep
with an unearthly passion
on the mouth

Sickness and reality were a
blur to the mortician
as he stared off into nothing
while washing his hands
after a midnight rally:

And so
the days, the nights
the evils, all came to
rest

Whisper the void

Hear the sound of my breath,
as only I am speaking to you
now

For a near moment, you must
know and hear the breath
as it passes my lips

I have seen the death of a
thousand lives
the birth of a million worlds
and the collapsed
stars being pulled out of the
plasma, from deep within
the annals of time

A spark, I tell you, can be seen
in all things
and it is the Maker who delivers
the spark
into all living things

What I speak of here is creation,
and I have been around long
enough to have seen it all,
and in every possible way

To look through these eyes
to have been witness
to over a billion years

to have known creation
to have witnessed death
and all the cycles that
life is capable
of being

I, am your witness
As it is I, who is your
story teller today,
for those who can not
ever remember that
which is from where they came

the spark and
the divinity
the first breath
the last life lived
the moments in between
the echos from the void
by the Maker

So be still now you child of man
and be quick
capture that butterfly in your
two hands

Look into its eyes
and see what is
your own reflection
as your time will always
be an endless loop
folding into a Oneness
The Singularity

Why so mean

Please,
please take me home
she says

Sitting in the corner of
a home, the stranger's house
in a white dress
knees pressed to her chest
spider webs calling from
above, no safety in sight

Please,
please let me go she says
I didn't mean to come here
and he just stares back,
all cold and vacant

You,
you are to be my pet!
No she cries, I need to go
home, my mother, my father
they will miss me!

No, he says
you are to be my pet,
spoken through a
face of chiseled stone

But yes! and then no!
Blood colored the walls
like a sort of mural
a Picasso from Hell

People thought, and people
did wonder, where she went
off to?

Was it a boy, was she unhappy?
No it was the ride she took with
the stranger, that had ended it all

For the virgin in the white dress

Rubbing your eyes

There is a fat old man
who beats a boy
with his cane
on Tuesdays

There is a boy who is now a man
who punishes an even older man
who is in a bed, fat and maligned
by paralysis on Wednesdays

Both times this happened,
it was raining on a Friday
all while
the clouds appeared luminous
speaking overhead
tossing thoughts
into my mind

and as I sit here, my wife is sitting
across from me, over there
just watching me write this crazy curve
drinking vodka, cold, in a glass
straight, no chaser

Sleep light

There are many hours
to the soul
and my eyes open
to see a bright light
appearing at the foot
of my bed
this night

Was it a car?
a flash light?
someone playing
a joke?
I think not

No, it is a sign
that those who give
prayer to The Oneness
are never wasting
their breath

Moving through a linear
time, walking through
the vessel of flesh and
blood, many hours will
be spent in thought:

Thinking of one's
own existence
thinking of one's
effect upon the world
thinking of one's own
voice among all the
other worldly noises

The soul is not singular
the soul is not to be owned
and the soul is not to be
ever fully understood,
of that I am certain

As you are human, you need
to realize that
you are all people
at all times and in all places
and
there is no separation,
that is just an illusion
in this world

Straight to Hell

Two men,
are to defy death tonight
as the
hot red tracers fly by their heads
lighting up the dead,
the dead of night

Up to their knees in mud
on their knees in mud
in the pouring rain,
such is the blight
of the green soldier
tonight

Who is an Uncle Tom
or maybe
an Uncle Sam
in the night
of death
behind us

Whisper Head

Wave that flag at me
just one more time
so tightly folded
with never a wrinkle,
unless you're a traitor
and
just one time
while all will be
laid to rest tonight
as hot red tracers
whiz by our heads
tonight
with our knees
in the jungle mud
Tonight,
it is tonight I tell you
maybe our last
night

Steak for lunch

The dog is so loyal
to me
while the cat
it gives me
zero respect,
none

I sit at the table
eating steak for
lunch with my kid
as this day is so good
to me

And all while the vegetarian
is away at work
not bearing witness
to the carnage

I'm eating and reading
at the same time
and in an instant the cat
has stepped across
my book and is going
for my steak

Whisper Head

My eyes are red with rage

Have you ever seen a
cat fly? This one does,
as I send him in the other
direction

At least when the dog
comes, he gives me sad
eyes, plays with my
heart strings
Yes, of course
you can have some
sympathy steak
my friend

The edge of me

Today,
I opened a door
and walked out of
my life

I gave no notice
and
no one knew
that I had quit
like it were a job
that I did

But tomorrow,
I shall walk back in
and take them all by
surprise and they won't
see it coming

They'll all ask me,
why I did it
was it a dirty trick
and did you mean it?

Of course I did,
I'd reply
for nothing is worth
keeping if you don't
ever test its boundaries
and know where it ever
ends

What I speak of is the
breath of man
and on Friday
I may just disappear again
but maybe
just maybe
I'll leave
a small
yellow post-it
saying:
farewell
this time
and
good bye

The eye of Lincoln

In my hands, I hold the steel
In my hands, I grip the handle
with my two working hands
I will swing and work the ax
for the fallen

I swing at a tree
but it has already fallen
I am too late now
but still I chase its
frozen and cold
branches, they will run
as only I have, can and will
until I've been able,
been able to weather this storm

This storm, it will come for all of us
very soon it shall come
and as the trunk lay at our feet
we shall see what has been
taken from us:
simple freedom
simple Liberty
and
we shall see what was stolen
from us, the American people

Whisper Head

Now, I hold the ax!
and I am ready to swing again
and remove what is yours
and you shall not take it from me
never again will you come to our shores
As I stand here free
for Liberty, until the death

Birth of me

In the dark, in a fluid world
a heartbeat can be heard
and
in the dark fluid of the universe
the breath of creation can be felt

The mother sits still
waiting for the first kick
and
the universe breathes as one voice
her message is heard
throughout time

Both the man and the woman
have joined, to create a life
and
God, as the universe is
starts with one singular thought
which is the seed
for all creation

As the two souls are united
one life force is passed to the next
and
as the hand of creation is felt
across time-space
the microbes begin to move
as the first signs of life
appear

The One gave life, as is
so that two may create one
as a ripple effect, bringing
the light from the darkness

The original thought
is the original sin

Titles by Author Craig Lefebvre:

The Vessel of ONE -book 1

Blue Star Prophecy -book 2

The Alien Abduction Survival Journal

Abductee Poetry

Button Factory (Poetry)

More information at www.dimensional-healings.com

E-mail: dimensional.healingsCT@gmail.com

Made in the USA
Middletown, DE
22 December 2020